Answer Book

Money and Finance

Information Handling

Time

Measure

Shape, Position and Movement

Contents

Contents

Money and Finance Pupil Book 4

Page 3
Airport prices

The best deal is shown in bold

1. BCP costs £157·50, **Kwik costs £150**, Supa costs £195 'example'
2. **BCP costs £135**, Kwik costs £136, Supa costs £195
3. BCP costs £210, Kwik costs £200, **Supa costs £195**
4. **BCP costs £82·50**, Kwik costs £86, Supa costs £195
5. BCP costs £165, **Kwik costs £159**, Supa costs £195
6. It is best to use Supa parking when you need between 26 and 35 days parking but not when it is exactly 28 days

Page 4
Phone calls

Cheapest is in bold

1. Cheap talk £0·96, Fast-chat £1·05, **Chat-chat £0·55.** 'example'
2. Cheap talk £1·44, Fast-chat £1·47, **Chat-chat £0·77**
3. **Cheap talk £1·68, Fast-chat £1·68,** Chat-chat £2·40
4. Cheap talk £2·64, **Fast-chat £2·52,** Chat-chat £3·60
5. Cheap talk £3·36, **Fast-chat £3·15,** Chat-chat £4·50
6. £10·60 + £12·60 = £23·20
£23·20 plus 20% VAT = £27·84

Page 5
Prices

1. £0·75 per 100 g 'example'
2. £1 per 100 g
3. £0·72 per 100 g
4. £0·18 per 100 g
5. £0·10 per 100 g
6. £0·10 per 100 g
7. £0·30 per 100 ml 'example'
8. £0·09 per 100 ml
9. £0·12 per 100 ml
10. £0·11 per 100 ml
11. £0·10 per 100 ml
12. £0·10 per 100 ml
Rocket Offer 8 is best.

Page 6
Value for money

1. b 'example'
2. b
3. a
4. a

5. Mrs Ahmed may think the large quantities of milk will go off before she gets to use them.
Rocket Answers may vary.

Page 7
Which is cheaper?

1. b by 80p 'example'
2. a by 84p
3. b by £1·22
4. b by £1·37
5. a by 34p
6. b by £6·53
7. £4·96 cheaper
8. 87p cheaper
Rocket Answers will vary.

Page 8
Can I afford it?

1. Yes, 8p left. 'example'
2. No. I need £1 more
3. No. I need £9·27 more
4. Yes, 1p left
5. No

Page 9
Can I afford it?

1. Yes. She will have £1·01 left. 'example'
2. No
3. Yes. She will have £2·01 left.
4. No
5. No
6. No
Rocket Yes

Page 10
Credit card statements

1. £326·00
2. £295·00
3. £44·25
4. £339·25
5. £44·25
Rocket Answers will vary.

Page 11
Money words

1. statement 'example'
2. borrow
3. pension
4. loan, interest
5. save, account
Rocket Answers will vary.

Page 12
Savings

1. £137·26
2. £112·26
3. A cheque for £25 was cashed

4. £40 was withdrawn from a cash machine
5. £17·26
6. £23·89
7. £6·00
Rocket £138·92

Page 13
Balances

1. Balance on 20th July £46·70
2. £285·55
3. £250·00
Rocket Answers will vary.

Page 14
Currencies

1. James bought the box of chocolates. 'example'
2. Chloe bought the pen
3. Susie bought the teddy
4. Raz bought the pearl necklace
5. Deepa bought the watch
6. Kit bought the t-shirt
7. Fiona bought the camera
Rocket £206

Page 15
Currencies

x-axis (£)	y-axis (Rupees)
1	80
2	160
3	240
4	320
5	400
6	480
7	560
8	640
9	720
10	800

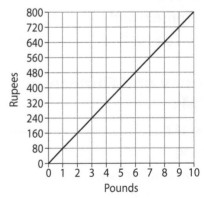

1. £10
2. £3
3. £5·50
4. £7
5. £6
6. £4·50
7. £9·50
8. £10

9. £2·50
10. 240 R
11. 400 R
12. 800 R
13. 200 R
14. 1200 R
15. 600 R
16. 3200 R
Rocket £125 000

Page 16
Currencies

1. 326 US dollars 'example'
2. 171 Euros
3. 66 000 Yen
4. £152·50
5. £264
6. £900
7. 46 200 Yen
8. 216·60 Euros
9. £2200
Rocket Answers will vary.

Page 17
Profit or loss?

1. £45 profit
2. £3·75 loss
3. £32 profit
4. £1·80 profit
5. 30p loss
Rocket Answers will vary.

Page 18
Enterprise decisions

1. £30
2. 151 (150 to break even)
3. £18
4. 180
5. 100%
6. £23·50

Page 19
Enterprise report

Answers will vary.

Money and Finance PPMs

PPM 142
Paying

1–5. Answers will vary.

PPM 143
Tickets, vouchers, receipts

Answers may vary but the following answers are most likely:
1. Throw away 'example'
2. Keep
3. Throw away
4. Keep
5. Keep
6. Keep
7. Keep

PPM 144
Taking care

1–7. Answers will vary.

PPM 145
Goods and services

1. Services 'example'
2. Goods
3. Services
4. Services
5. Services
6. Goods
7–9. Answers will vary.

PPM 146
Needs and wants

1–7. Answers will vary.

PPM 147
Spending

1 and 2. Answers will vary.

PPM 148
How much?

1. £5·99
2. £14·95
3. £89
4. £1250
5. £8·49
6. £35
7. £9789
8. £130 000
9. Answers will vary.

PPM 149
You choose

1–7. Answers will vary.

PPM 150
Worth it

1. Car 'example'
2–7. Answers will vary.

PPM 151
Total cost

1. Missing numbers:
   £130, £220, Subtotal £350,
   VAT £70, Total £420
2. Missing numbers:
   £120, £70, Subtotal £190, VAT £38,
   Total £228
3. £60

PPM 152
Which shop?

1. £277·99, £282·74
2. £279·99, £285·48
3. £280·25, £280·25
4. If he gets the camera and batteries from Hanleys and flashcard from Murrys he would pay £273·48.

PPM 153
Special offers

1. 3 for 2 costs £6. Other costs £6·50 so the first offer is cheaper by 50p.
2. 3 for 2 costs £2·40. Other costs £3 so the first offer is cheaper by 60p.
3. 3 for 2 costs £1·12. Other costs £1 so the second offer is cheaper by 12p.

PPM 154
Budgeting

1. Answers will vary.
2. Answers will vary.

PPM 155
Budgeting

1. Answers will vary.

PPM 156
Living within a budget

Answers will vary according to whether children count a month as four weeks or work out the incomes and expenses per year. The following is based on the four weeks = 1 month model.
1. £692
2. £530·27
3. Answers will vary.

PPM 157
Spreading payments

1. £35 more
2. £47 more
3. £10 less
4. £22 less

PPM 158
Bank statement

1. Missing balances:
   1600, 1400, 1365, 1265, 1248·25,
   1227·25, 1627·25, 1569·80,
   1319·80
   Final four boxes:
   £1400·00
   £680·20
   £600·00
   £1319·80

PPM 159

Bank statement

1. Missing balances:
   410, 310, 265, 75, –25, –44, –74, 11, –119
   Final four boxes:
   £535
   £614
   –£40
   –£119

PPM 160

Bank statement

1. Answers will vary but the amounts paid in should total £50 and the amounts paid out should total £589·60

PPM 161

Currencies

1. 50p 'example'
2. 75p
3. £1·25
4. £1·75
5. £2·00
6. £3·00
7. £11·00
8. £25·00
9. 9
10. 15
11. 36
12. 40
13. 41
14. 31

24 blob perfume bottle: £6·00, 33 blob perfume bottle: £8·25, 17 blob perfume bottle: £4·25, 52 blob perfume bottle: £13·00, 19 blob perfume bottle: £4·75

PPM 162

Currencies

1–10. Answers will vary according to exchange rate.

PPM 163

Enterprise project

1 and 2. Answers will vary.

PPM 164

Your dream project

Answers will vary.

PPM 165

Accounts

Answers will vary.

PPM 166

Evaluation

Answers will vary.

Information Handling Pupil Book 4

Page 20

Grouping data

1.

Cups	1–2	3–4	5–6	7–8	9–10	11–12
Tallies	|||	卌 卌	卌 |||	||||	|||	||

2.

Cups	1–2	3–4	5–6	7–8	9–10	11–12
Frequency	3	10	8	4	3	2

3.

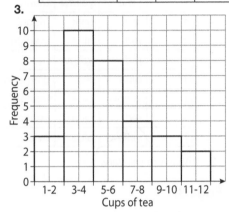

4. 3–4
5. 11–12
6. 9
7. 3
8. 22
9. False

Page 21

Grouping data

1. In fives
2. 11–15 packets
3. 22 children
4. 4 children
5. 88 children
6. 1–30
7. 35 children
8. 12 children
9. 63 children

Rocket Answers will vary.

Page 22

Bar graphs

1. 0·7 kg
2. 1·7 kg
3. 0·9 kg
4. 1·9 kg
5. 1·3 kg
6. 1·7 kg
7. Monday, Tuesday, Wednesday, Thursday
8. 0·2 kg
9. 0·9 kg
10. 1·7 kg
11. 3·2 kg
12. 5 kg
13. 6·9 kg
14. Answers will vary.

Rocket Answers will vary.

Page 23

Bar line graphs

1. 35 dogs 'example'
2. 45 dogs
3. 5 dogs
4. 1 puppy; 15 dogs had litters of this size
5. 9 puppies; 5 dogs had litters of this size
6. 65 dogs
7. 80 dogs
8. 150 dogs
9. Answers will vary.

Rocket Answers will vary.

Page 24

Bar line charts

1.

Temperature	10°	11°	12°	13°	14°	15°	16°
Frequency	1	3	6	10	4	3	1

2.

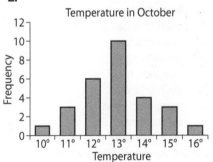

Rocket Answers will vary.

Page 25

Probability

Answers to questions 1–16 may vary.

1. Impossible
2. Unlikely/Likely
3. Certain/Impossible (for children with walking difficulties)
4. Unlikely
5. Impossible
6. Unlikely
7. Unlikely
8. Likely
9. Unlikely

10. Impossible
11. Unlikely/Likely
12. Likely
13. Unlikely/Likely
14. Unlikely/Likely
15. Unlikely/Likely
16. Impossible
First Rocket Answers will vary.
Second Rocket Answers may vary.

Page 26
Probability

Answers to questions 1–9 may vary.
1. No chance 'example'
2. Answers may vary.
3. Good chance
4. Answers may vary.
5. Good chance
6. Answers may vary.
7. Answers may vary.
8. No chance
9. Answers will vary.
10. Even
11. Poor chance
12. Poor chance
13. Even chance
14. No chance
15. Even chance
16. Good chance
17. Certain
18. Good chance

Page 27
Probability

1. less than even 'example'
2. even chance
3. even chance
4. even chance
5. certain
6. less than even
7. even chance
8. more than even
9. even chance
10. less than even
Rocket Answers will vary.

Page 28
Questionnaires

Answers will vary.

Page 29
Questionnaires

Answers will vary.

Page 30
Databases

1.

Flower	Central colour	Petal colour	Petal shape	Number of petals
a	red	yellow	oval	8
b	yellow	red	triangle	6
c	red	blue	diamond	4
d	yellow	blue	oval	8
e	yellow	yellow	triangle	6
f	red	pink	triangle	6
g	red	blue	triangle	8
h	red	yellow	oval	4
i	blue	red	diamond	4
j	yellow	blue	triangle	8
k	red	blue	square	4
l	yellow	blue	oval	12

2. Answers will vary.

Page 31
Databases

1–4. Answers will vary.

Page 32
Sorting

1. Answers will vary.
2. 24 shapes as follows:
   circle red large thin
   circle red large thick
   circle red small thin
   circle red small thick
   circle yellow large thin
   circle yellow large thick
   circle yellow small thin
   circle yellow small thick
   triangle red large thin
   triangle red large thick
   triangle red small thin
   triangle red small thick
   triangle yellow large thin
   triangle yellow large thick
   triangle yellow small thin
   triangle yellow small thick
   square red large thin
   square red large thick
   square red small thin
   square red small thick
   square yellow large thin
   square yellow large thick
   square yellow small thin
   square yellow small thick
3. Answers will vary.
Rocket An extra 12 shapes would be added.

Page 33
Pie charts

1. $\frac{1}{12}$ 'example'
2. $\frac{2}{12}$ or $\frac{1}{6}$
3. $\frac{1}{12}$
4. $\frac{4}{12}$ or $\frac{1}{3}$
5. $\frac{3}{12}$ or $\frac{1}{4}$
6. $\frac{5}{12}$
7. $\frac{9}{12}$ or $\frac{3}{4}$
8. $\frac{5}{12}$
9. 20
10. 40
11. 30
12. 30
13. 30
14. 0
Rocket Answers will vary. If 16 friends are surveyed, each wedge represents 2 people.

Page 34
Pie charts

1. $\frac{3}{12}$ or $\frac{1}{4}$
2. $\frac{2}{12}$ or $\frac{1}{6}$
3. $\frac{9}{12}$ or $\frac{3}{4}$
4. $\frac{2}{12}$ or $\frac{1}{6}$
5. $\frac{3}{12}$ or $\frac{1}{4}$
6. $\frac{4}{12}$ or $\frac{1}{3}$
7. 60
8. 30
9. 90
10. 270
11. 270
12. 60
13. Answers will vary.
Rocket Answers will vary.

Page 35

Pie charts

1.

Word length	1–3	4–6	7–9	10–12
Number of words	2	6	8	4

2. pink 'example'
3. yellow **4.** green **5.** blue
6. 8 **7.** 4
Rocket Answers will vary.

Page 36

Line graphs

1. 50 cm
2. 30 cm
3. 170 cm
4. 190 cm
5. May
6. August, September, October
7. Answers will vary.
Rocket Answers will vary.

Page 37

Line graphs

1. 04:00–06:00, 00:00
2. 08:00, 22:00
3. 12:00, 18:00
4. 10:00, 20:00
5. 14:00
6. 13:00, 16:00
7. 14:00
8. 04:00–06:00, 00:00
9. 11:00, 19:00
10. 10° **11.** 11° **12.** 14°
13. 10° **14.** 11° **15.** 16°
16. 20° **17.** 16°
Rocket Answers will vary.

Page 38

Line graphs

1.

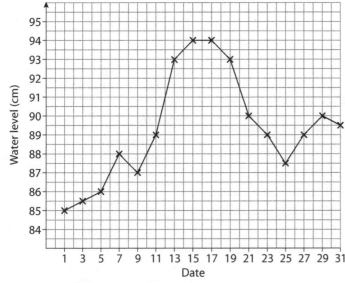

2. 15 March to 17 March

3. 1st March
4. 31st March
5. 91 cm
6. 89·5 cm
7. 89·5 cm
Rocket Answers will vary.

Page 39

Line graphs

1. $32 **2.** $80 **3.** $128
4. $113 **5.** $73 **6.** £20
7. £49 **8.** £59 **9.** £39
10. £16
Rocket Answers will vary.

Page 40

Probability

1. one in ten, $\frac{1}{10}$ 'example'
2. one in ten, $\frac{1}{10}$
3. six in ten, $\frac{6}{10}$ or $\frac{3}{5}$
4. two in ten, $\frac{2}{10}$ or $\frac{1}{5}$
5. two in ten, $\frac{2}{10}$ or $\frac{1}{5}$
6. five in ten, $\frac{5}{10}$ or $\frac{1}{2}$
7. none, 0
8. five in ten, $\frac{5}{10}$ or $\frac{1}{2}$
9. three in ten, $\frac{3}{10}$
10. four in ten, $\frac{4}{10}$ or $\frac{2}{5}$
11. two in ten, $\frac{2}{10}$ or $\frac{1}{5}$
12. four in ten, $\frac{4}{10}$ or $\frac{2}{5}$
13. false
14. false
15. false
16. true
Rocket Answers will vary.

Page 41

Probability

1. $\frac{3}{10}$ **2.** $\frac{2}{10}$ or $\frac{1}{5}$
3. $\frac{1}{10}$ **4.** $\frac{5}{10}$ or $\frac{2}{5}$
5. $\frac{7}{10}$ **6.** $\frac{4}{10}$ or $\frac{2}{5}$
7. $\frac{5}{10}$ or $\frac{1}{2}$ **8.** $\frac{9}{10}$
9. $\frac{7}{10}$ **10.** $\frac{3}{10}$
11. $\frac{0}{10}$

First Rocket Answers will vary.
Second Rocket There is a $\frac{4}{10}$ or $\frac{2}{5}$ chance of taking a prime number from cards 1–10; $\frac{8}{20}$ or $\frac{2}{5}$ chance in cards 1–20; $\frac{10}{30}$ or $\frac{1}{3}$ chance in cards 1–30; $\frac{12}{40}$ or $\frac{3}{10}$ chance in cards 1–40; $\frac{15}{50}$ or $\frac{3}{10}$ chance in cards 1–50; $\frac{17}{60}$ chance in cards 1–60; $\frac{19}{70}$ chance in cards 1–70; $\frac{22}{80}$ or $\frac{11}{40}$ chance in cards 1–80; $\frac{24}{90}$ or $\frac{4}{15}$ chance in cards 1–90; $\frac{25}{100}$ or $\frac{1}{4}$ chance in cards 1–100.

Page 42

Probability

1. $\frac{1}{2}$ **2.** $\frac{1}{4}$
3. $\frac{1}{4}$ **4.** $\frac{1}{2}$
5. $\frac{4}{10}$ or $\frac{2}{5}$ **6.** $\frac{2}{40}$ or $\frac{1}{20}$
7. $\frac{8}{40}$ or $\frac{1}{5}$ **8.** $\frac{10}{40}$ or $\frac{1}{4}$
9. $\frac{20}{40}$ or $\frac{1}{2}$ **10.** $\frac{2}{40}$ or $\frac{1}{20}$
11. $\frac{10}{40}$ or $\frac{1}{4}$ **12.** 0
13. $\frac{30}{40}$ or $\frac{3}{4}$ **14.** $\frac{8}{40}$ or $\frac{1}{5}$
15. $\frac{1}{40}$ **16.** $\frac{20}{40}$ or $\frac{1}{2}$
17. Answers will vary.
Rocket Answers will vary.

Page 43

Medians

1. 1, 1, 2, 3, 3, 4, 4, 5, 7
Median = 3
2. 1, 1, 2, 2, 3, 4, 5
Median = 2
3. 1, 2, 2, 3, 3, 4, 5, 5
Median = 3
4. 1, 2, 2, 3, 4, 6, 6, 7, 8, 9
Median = 5
5. 1, 1, 2, 2, 3, 3, 4, 4
Median = 2·5
6. 2, 3, 5, 5, 5, 5, 5, 6, 7, 9
Median = 5
7. The last score could have been 7, 8, 9 or 10.

Page 44

Averages

1. 5 + 7 + 4 + 7 + 7 = 30
  30 ÷ 5 = 6
2. 8 + 2 + 7 + 4 + 4 = 25
  25 ÷ 5 = 5
3. 3 + 2 + 5 + 4 + 4 + 6 = 24
  24 ÷ 6 = 4
4. 8 + 7 + 7 + 6 = 28
  28 ÷ 4 = 7
5. 6 + 10 + 8 + 9 + 9 + 9 + 5 = 56
  56 ÷ 7 = 8

6. $4 + 3 + 6 + 5 + 5 + 7 = 30$
$30 \div 6 = 5$

7. $6 + 6 + 8 + 7 + 9 + 6 = 42$
$42 \div 6 = 7$

8. $2 + 1 + 3 + 7 + 4 + 6 + 5 + 8 + 2 + 1 = 39$
Mean = 3·9

9. $4 + 3 + 4 + 2 + 3 + 4 + 2 + 3 + 4 + 2 = 31$
Mean = 3·1

10. $6 + 6 + 3 + 6 + 3 + 6 + 7 + 10 + 7 + 3 = 57$
Mean = 5·7

11. $9 + 9 + 2 + 8 + 12 + 10 + 3 + 3 + 6 + 10 = 72$
Mean = 7·2

12. $4 + 4 + 8 + 10 + 4 + 3 + 6 + 9 + 2 + 7 = 57$
Mean = 5·7

13. $12 + 15 + 11 + 12 + 22 + 13 + 12 + 9 + 11 + 15 = 132$
Mean = 13·2

14. In order: Guy, Cho, Peter, Beth, Dan, Ramesh

Rocket Answers will vary.

Page 45

Averages

1. a) 6·5°C
 b) 7°C
 c) 7°C
2. a) 6·2°C
 b) 6°C
 c) 6°C
3. a) 19·1°C
 b) 18°C
 c) 19°C
4. a) 12·6°C
 b) 12°C
 c) 12·5°C
5. a) 6·5°C
 b) 6 or 7°C
 c) 6·5°C
6. a) 11·5°C
 b) 12°C
 c) 11·5°C
7. a) 27·7°C
 b) 28°C
 c) 28°C
8. a) 34·5°C
 b) 33°C
 c) 34·5°C
9. 5
10. 7
11. 7
12. 14
13. 31
14. 30
Rocket Mean 30·4 days; median 31 days; mode 31 days. In a leap year mean 30·5 days; median and mode the same as before.

Page 46

Find out and show

1–4. Answers will vary.

Page 47

Find out and show

1–6. Answers will vary.
Rocket Answers will vary.

Information Handling PPMs

PPM 167

Tally chart

Vowel	Frequency
a	17
e	24
i	16
o	12
u	8

1. 17 **2.** 8 **3.** 12
4. e **5.** u **6.** 40
7. 29 **8.** 57 **9.** 36

PPM 168

Frequency table

Digit	0	1	2	3	4	5	6	7	8	9
Frequency	6	4	7	4	2	6	3	3	4	5

1. 5 **2.** 2
3. 7 **4.** 4

PPM 169

Grouped data

1. 6–10 **2.** 21–25
3. 16–20 **4.** 11–15
5. 3 **6.** 9
7. 19 **8.** 14
9. 25 **10.** 28
11. 32 **12.** 14
13. 46 **14.** 47
15. 60

PPM 170

Grouped data

Minutes	Tally	Frequency
0–15	|||	3
16–30	ЖЖ ЖЖ |||	13
31–45	ЖЖ ЖЖ		11
46–60	ЖЖ ||	7
61–75	ЖЖ |||	8
76–90	ЖЖ ЖЖ ||||	14

PPM 171

Pictogram

1. 6 **2.** 16 **3.** 13
4. 7 **5.** 9 **6.** 3
7. 9 **8.** 6 **9.** 7

PPM 172

Bar graphs

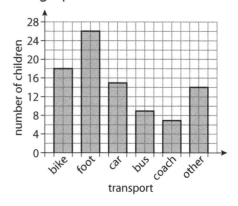

PPM 173

Bar graphs

1. 29 **2.** 26 **3.** 28
4. 27 **5.** 24 **6.** 25
7. 25 **8.** 23
9. Y3 5; Y4 4 **10.** Y3 6; Y4 3

PPM 174

Dice bar line graph

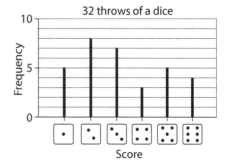

PPM 175

Goals bar line graph

1. 9 **2.** 3 **3.** 10
4. 4 **5.** 6 **6.** 5
7. 9 **8.** 7 **9.** 4
10. 16 **11.** 18 **12.** 80

PPM 176

Venn diagrams

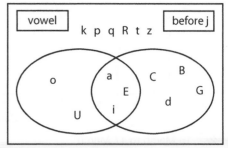

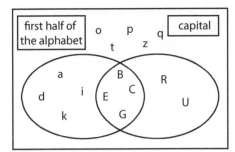

PPM 177

Carroll diagrams

	even	not even
multiple of 5	10 20 50	5 15
not a multiple of 5	6 18 22	9 13 21

	digital total less than 10	digital total not less than 10
even	14 32 42 60	28 48 56 74
not even	17 35 81	55 75 95

	multiple of 3	not a multiple of 3
multiple of 2	6 18 42	4 8 14 28 32
not a multiple of 2	3 15 21	7 11 13 17 23

PPM 178

Tree diagram

1. Box 1: 56, 60, 61, 62, 63, 64
   Box 2: 50, 51, 52, 53, 54, 55, 57, 58, 59
   Box 3: 65, 66, 67, 68, 69, 76
   Box 4: 70, 71, 72, 73, 74, 75, 77, 78, 79, 80
2. Box 1: 110, 111, 112, 113, 114, 115
   Box 2: 88, 99, 100, 101,
   Box 3: 103, 104, 105, 106, 107, 108, 109
   Box 4: 87, 89, 90, 91, 92, 93, 94, 95, 96, 97, 98, 102
3. Answers will vary.

PPM 179

Carroll and Venn diagrams

1.

	50 or more	not 50 or more
digit total is 12 or more	75 84 97	48 39 49
digit total is not 12 or more	50 65 62 81	20 40 17

2.

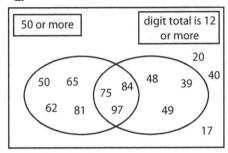

3. Answers will vary.

PPM 180

Carroll, Venn and tree diagrams

Answers will vary.

PPM 181

Three criteria

1 and 2. Answers will vary.

PPM 182

Chance line

Answers may vary.

PPM 183

Chances

1–10. Answers will vary.
11. Answers will vary but should follow some order such as:
   certain 'example'
   very likely
   probable/likely
   even chance/fair chance
   possible
   unlikely/poor chance
   very unlikely
   impossible

PPM 184

Questionnaire

1 and 2. Answers will vary.

PPM 185

Database

1.

Creature	Is it a bird?	Does it fly?
ostrich	Yes	No
sparrow	Yes	Yes
bat	No	Yes
cat	No	No
robin	Yes	Yes
penguin	Yes	No
dog	No	No
blackbird	Yes	Yes
butterfly	No	Yes
magpie	Yes	Yes
wasp	No	Yes
emu	Yes	No
bee	No	Yes
worm	No	No

2. ostrich, penguin, emu
3. bat, butterfly, wasp, bee
4.

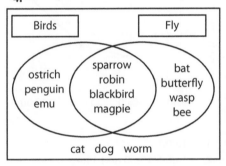

PPM 186

Database

1. chaffinch 15 cm 30 g
   goldcrest 9 cm 6 g
   mistle thrush 27 cm 99 g
   blackbird 26 cm 100 g
   treecreeper 12 cm 10 g
   great tit 14 cm 17 g
2–3. Answers will vary.

PPM 187

Pie chart

1–4. Answers will vary.

PPM 188

Pie charts

1. adventure   2. soaps
3. 6   4. 8   5. 2
6. 3   7. 5   8. 3
9. $\frac{5}{16}$ 10. $\frac{6}{16}$ or $\frac{3}{8}$
11. $\frac{2}{16}$ or $\frac{1}{8}$

PPM 189

Pie charts

1 and 2. Answers will vary.

3. Answers may vary but should include: on the first chart each segment represents 2 dice rolls. On the second chart each segment represents 3 dice rolls. The two charts can be used to compare fractions ('The first time we got a 5 $\frac{1}{6}$ of the time and the second time we got it more than $\frac{1}{6}$ of the time'). But it can be misleading to use them to compare absolute numbers because, say, 4 dice rolls look differently on the two charts.

PPM 190
Pie charts

Answers will vary.

PPM 191
Line graph

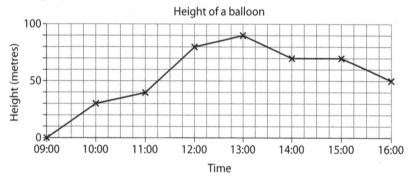

Height of a balloon

1. 13:00
2. 14:00–15:00 and 11:45
3. Times between 09:00 and 13:00
4. Times between 13:00 and 14:00; and times between 15:00 and 16:00
5. rising
6. descending

PPM 192
Dice probabilities

1.	$\frac{1}{6}$ 'example'	**2.**	$\frac{1}{6}$
3.	$\frac{3}{6}$ or $\frac{1}{2}$	**4.**	$\frac{3}{6}$ or $\frac{1}{2}$
5.	$\frac{4}{6}$ or $\frac{2}{3}$	**6.**	$\frac{2}{6}$ or $\frac{1}{3}$
7.	$\frac{2}{6}$ or $\frac{1}{3}$	**8.**	$\frac{2}{6}$ or $\frac{1}{3}$
9.	$\frac{2}{6}$ or $\frac{1}{3}$	**10.**	$\frac{4}{6}$ or $\frac{2}{3}$
11.	$\frac{4}{6}$ or $\frac{2}{3}$	**12.**	$\frac{4}{6}$ or $\frac{2}{3}$
13.	$\frac{2}{6}$ or $\frac{1}{3}$	**14.**	$\frac{1}{6}$
15.	$\frac{3}{6}$ or $\frac{1}{2}$	**16.**	$\frac{5}{6}$
17.	$\frac{4}{6}$ or $\frac{2}{3}$	**18.**	$\frac{2}{6}$ or $\frac{1}{3}$

PPM 193
Probability line

1. a cross at $\frac{2}{6}$
2. a cross at $\frac{4}{6}$
3. a cross at $\frac{1}{2}$
4. a cross at $\frac{1}{8}$
5. a cross at $\frac{1}{10}$
6. a cross at $\frac{4}{10}$
7. a cross at $\frac{1}{5}$
8. a cross at $\frac{5}{8}$ on a line with 8 intervals
9. a cross at $\frac{3}{10}$ on a line with 10 intervals

PPM 194
Mean averages

1.	6 'example'	**2.**	8
3.	14	**4.**	22
5.	5	**6.**	11
7.	10	**8.**	9
9.	50	**10.**	28
11.	5	**12.**	7·5
13.	4	**14.**	13·25
15.	5·75	**16.**	5·25
17.	9·5	**18.**	10

PPM 195
Dice averages

1–5. Answers will vary.

PPM 196
Mean, mode, median and range

1. 2, 2 'example'
2. 3, 3
3. any two numbers
4. any numbers where the difference between the smallest and largest is 6
5. any numbers whose total is 11
6. 9 (as there are only 6 cards the median is halfway between 7 and 9)
7. Answers will vary.

PPM 197
Collecting data

Answers will vary.

Time Pupil Book 5

Page 3
Calendars

1. Winter: December, January, February
   Spring: March, April, May
   Summer: June, July, August
   Autumn: September, October, November
2. 1st June
3. 7th June
4. 8th June
5. 4th June
6. 12th June
7. 10th June

Rocket Answers will vary.

Page 4
Calendars

1. 5 Tuesdays
2. Mondays
3. Wednesday 3rd September
4. 4 days
5. Twice: September 6th and 14th
6. 2 days
7. Friday 12th September

Rocket Answers will vary.

Page 5
Time

1. second, minute, hour, day, week, fortnight, month, year
2. second, minute
3. year
4. fortnight
5. second, minute, hour, day
6. hour
7. fortnight, month
8. hours and/or minutes
9. minutes
10. days or weeks
11. hours or minutes
12. years
13. months
14. seconds or minutes
15. hours or minutes

Rocket Answers will vary.

Page 6

Time

1. 4:00 pm 'example'
2. 12:50 am
3. 6:30 pm
4. 12:20 am
5. 6:00 am
6. 10:30 pm
7. 7:45 am
8. 2:25 pm
9. 5:55 pm
10. 3:15 pm
11. 00:14 'example'
12. 12:30
13. 11:50
14. 12:05
15. 11:34
16. 21:00

Rocket Answers will vary.

Page 7

Time

1. 19:05 'example'
2. 02:15   3. 18:42   4. 08:13
5. 06:45   6. 20:25   7. 09:53
8. 15:12   9. 16:30   10. 05:35
11. False   12. True   13. True
14. False   15. False   16. True

Rocket Answers may vary.

Page 8

Time problems

1. 34 minutes 'example'
2. 1 hour 54 minutes
3. 5:20
4. 46 minutes
5. 9:30
6. 11:30
7. 25 minutes each

Rocket Answers will vary.

Page 9

Time problems

1. 38 minutes 'example'
2. 7:18 am
3. 45 minutes
4. $2\frac{1}{2}$ hours
5. 11:32 am
6. 1 hour 15 minutes or 75 minutes

Rocket Answers will vary.

Page 10

Time problems

1. 2 hours and 20 minutes 'example'
2. 1:40 pm or 13:40
3. 2:20 pm or 14:20
4. 3:15 pm or 15:15
5. 36 minutes
6. 4:21 pm or 16:21
7. 29 minutes

8. 5:15 pm or 17:15

Rocket Answers will vary.

Page 11

Timetables

1.

Snoreton	Little Boring	Sleepville	Dozetown	Snoozeford
10:15	10:32	10:54	11:03	11:26
12:04	12:21	12:43	12:52	13:15
14:43	15:00	15:22	15:31	15:54
17:30	17:47	18:09	18:18	18:41

2. 17 minutes 'example'
3. 22 minutes   4. 9 minutes
5. 23 minutes   6. 39 minutes
7. 31 minutes   8. 32 minutes
9. 54 minutes
10. 1 hour 11 minutes

Rocket Answers will vary.

Page 12

Timetables

1. 16:25, 18:25, 20:25
2. 10:30, 12:30, 14:30
3. 12:05, 14:05, 16:05
4. 17:05, 19:05, 21:05
5. 11:35, 13:35, 15:35
6. 18:35, 20:35, 22:35
7. 1 hour 35 minutes
8. 1 hour 35 minutes
9. 1 hour 5 minutes
10. 40 minutes

Rocket Answers will vary.

Page 13

Organising time

1 and **2**. Answers may vary.
Rocket Answers will vary.

Page 14

Organising time

	Monday	Tuesday	Wednesday	Thursday	Friday
3:15	Trumpet	Computer club		Art club	
3:30	Trumpet	Computer club	Football practice	Art club	Guitar
3:45	Swimming	Computer club	Football practice	Art club	Guitar
4:00	Swimming	Computer club	Football practice	Art club	Scouts
4:15	Swimming		Football practice		Scouts
4:30	Swimming	Gymnastics	Football practice		Scouts
4:45	Swimming	Gymnastics			Scouts
5:00	Swimming	Gymnastics	Orchestra		
5:15	Swimming		Orchestra		
5:30			Orchestra		
5:45					

Rocket Answers will vary.

Page 15

Time problems

1. 1   2. 1   3. 5
4. 2   5. 1   6. 1

Rocket Answers will vary.

Page 16

Speed

1. 10 miles   2. 20 miles
3. 30 miles   4. 60 miles
5. $1\frac{1}{2}$ miles   6. $7\frac{1}{2}$ miles
7. 12 miles   8. 1 mile
9. 10 miles   10. 5 miles
11. 1 mile   12. 15 miles
13. True   14. False
15. True

Page 17

Speed

1. $\frac{1}{4}$ hour 'example'
2. $1\frac{3}{4}$ hours or 1 hr 45 mins
3. $2\frac{1}{4}$ hours or 2 hrs 15 mins
4. $3\frac{1}{2}$ hours or 3 hrs 30 mins
5. $1\frac{1}{2}$ hours or 1 hr 30 mins
6. 2 hours
7. $\frac{1}{2}$ hour or 30 mins

8. $3\frac{1}{2}$ hours or 3 hr 30 mins
9. 4 hours
10. $\frac{1}{2}$ hour or 30 mins
11. 8 hours
12. 11 hours
13. 10 hours 'example'
14. 5 hours
15. 4 hours
16. 20 hours
Rocket 50 km per hour.

Page 18
Speed

1. Katy's plane (1 m in $\frac{1}{2}$ sec); Marie's car (1 m in 5 secs); (1 m in $\frac{1}{2}$ sec); Ben's car (1 m in 10 secs)
2. 80 kph 'example'
3. 48 kph
4. 112 kph
5. 72 kph

Page 19
Time

1. 04:00 'example'
2. 06:00
3. 11:00
4. 10:00
5. 03:00
6. 01:00
7. 05:00
8. 08:00
9. 17:00
10. 17:00
11. 09:00
12. 14:00
Rocket Answers will vary

Page 20
Time problems

1. Ali, Darren, Chrissie, Ba
2. 8·6 seconds
3. 5·2 seconds
4. 3 mins 10·3 seconds
5. 47·575 seconds
6. Ben or Chrissie
7. 3·9 seconds
8. About 4:48
9. 21 tenths
Rocket 4 mins 19 seconds

Time PPMs

PPM 198
Planning time

Answers may vary. The following are possible answers:
2 'example', 3, 6
1, 4, 5
Answers will vary.

PPM 199
Ages

1–7. Answers will vary according to age of child.

PPM 200
Which day?

1. Saturday 'example'
2. Wednesday
3. Tuesday
4. Sunday
5. Sunday
6. Tuesday
7.

May 2018						
Monday	Tuesday	Wednesday	Thursday	Friday	Saturday	Sunday
	1	2	3	4	5	6
7	8	9	10	11	12	13
14	15	16	17	18	19	20
21	22	23	24	25	26	27
28	29	30	31			

PPM 201
Estimate

1–11. Answers will vary.

PPM 202
Estimate

1–9. Answers will vary.

PPM 203
Estimate

1–10. Answers will vary.

PPM 204
Analogue and digital times

1. 1:27 'example'
2. 3:46
3. 5:09
4. 10:16
5. 8:22
6. 6:37
7. 5:47
8. 3:52
9. 4:58
10–12. Answers will vary.

PPM 205
Minute hand

1. 'example'

4:43

2.

3:36

3.

6:08

4.

7:52

5.

10:43

6.

5:17

7.

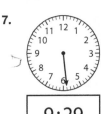

9:29

8.

1:03

9.

2:13

10.

12:28

11.

11:46

12.

8:57

PPM 206

How much?

1. 60 seconds
2. 15 seconds
3. 95 seconds
4. 150 seconds
5. 187 seconds
6. 600 seconds
7. 1 minute 30 seconds
8. 1 minute 5 seconds
9. 2 minutes 15 seconds
10. 3 minutes 20 seconds
11. 1 minute 40 seconds

PPM 207

Units of time

1. 120 seconds
2. 90 seconds
3. 300 seconds
4. 3600 seconds
5. 86 seconds
6. 60 minutes
7. 45 minutes
8. 30 minutes
9. 180 minutes
10. 177 minutes
11. 24 hours
12. 8 hours
13. 60 hours
14. 168 hours
15. 103 hours
16. 14 days
17. 2 days
18. 365 or 366 days
19. 30 days
20. 61 days

PPM 208

am and pm

Answers are likely to be:
1. Eating lunch
2. At school
3. In bed
4. Watching TV
5. In bed
6. Getting up
7. At school
8. Answers will vary.

PPM 209

Time trail

1. 8:00 pm
   4:00 pm
   1:30 pm
   1:45 pm
   1:50 pm
   11:50 am
   12:10 pm
   12:55 pm
   7:55 am
   9:00 am
   1:00 am
2. Answers will vary.

PPM 210

24 hour clock

1. 2:28 pm 'example'
2. 6:15 pm
3. 7:11 am
4. 11:45 am
5. 1:50 pm
6. 11:17 pm
7. 2:40 am
8. 10:20 pm
9. 9:09 am
10–12. Answers will vary.

PPM 211

24 hour clock

1. 20:24 'example'
2. 18:11
3. 14:41
4. 13:27
5. 16:53
6. 23:16
7. 20:09
8. 22:29
9. 17:03
10. 15:36
11. 21:13
12. 19:19

PPM 212

24 hour times

1.
   17:50 — Line to 'Ten to six in the evening'
   02:05 — Line to 'Five past two in the morning'
   14:05 — Line to 'Five past two in the afternoon'
   10:45 — Line to 'Quarter to eleven in the morning'
   15:30 — Line to 'Half past three in the afternoon'
   00:15 — Line to 'Twelve fifteen at night'
   20:55 — Line to 'Five to nine in the evening'
   12:15 — Line to 'Twelve fifteen at lunchtime'
   23:45 — Line to 'Quarter to midnight'
   07:20 — Line to 'Seven twenty in the morning'
2. 00:15, 02:05, 07:20, 10:45, 12:15, 14:05, 15:30, 17:50, 20:55, 23:45

PPM 213

Time differences

1. 3 hours
2. 40 minutes
3. 1 hour 40 minutes
4. 2 hours 35 minutes
5. 3 hours 35 minutes
6. 2 hours 25 minutes
7. 4 hours 40 minutes
8. 7 hours 20 minutes
9. Answers will vary.

PPM 214

Time differences

1. 1 hour 55 minutes
2. 3 hours 40 minutes

3. 45 minutes
4. 2 hours 35 minutes
5. 4 hours 21 minutes
6. 59 minutes
7. 2 hours 34 minutes
8. 3 hours 33 minutes
9. Answers will vary.

PPM 215
Timetable

Answers will vary.

PPM 216
Train timetable

2nd train	3rd train	4th train
10:25	14:05	19:16
10:37	14:17	19:28
10:46	14:26	19:37
11:11	14:51	20:02
11:27	15:07	20:18
11:48	15:28	20:39
12:03	15:43	20:54
12:22	16:02	21:13
12:38	16:18	21:29
12:57	16:37	21:48

PPM 217
Time zones

1–3. Answers will vary.

PPM 218
Time problems

1. 7 minutes
2. 20 hours 25 minutes
3. 9
4. $4\frac{1}{2}$ hours
5. 11:53 pm
6. 2 hours 32 minutes
7. Answers will vary.

Measure Pupil Book 5

Page 21
Estimating

Answers may vary but could be:
1. car, ladder, TV, bath, bucket
2. car, ladder, TV, bath, bucket
3. car, bath, bucket
4. teacup, needle, apple
5. teacup
6. teacup, needle, apple
7. car, ladder, bath
8. TV, bucket
9. teacup, needle, apple
Rocket Answers will vary.

Page 22
Estimating

1. 25 m 'example'
2. 2 litres
3. 35 g
4. 400 km
5. 10 g
6. 200 m
7. 8 kg
8. Answers will vary.

Page 23
Estimate

A. $5\frac{1}{2}$ cm
B. $7\frac{1}{2}$ cm
C. 7 cm
D. 4 cm
E. 3 cm
F. 10 cm
G. $8\frac{1}{2}$ cm
H. 4 cm
I. 11 cm
Rocket Answers will vary.

Page 24
Estimate

1–9. Answers will vary.
Rocket Answers will vary.

Page 25
Estimating distance

1–10. Answers will vary.
Rocket Answers will vary.
11. Approximately 10 cm.

Page 26
Weight

1. mouse: 20 g 'example'
2. rabbit: 3 kg
3. cat: 6 kg
4. dog: 10 kg
5. hamster: 700 g
6. stick insect: 5 g
Rocket Answers will vary.
7. 1250 g = $1\frac{1}{4}$ kg 'example'
8. 1000 g = 1 kg
9. 500 g = $\frac{1}{2}$ kg
10. 2500 g = $2\frac{1}{2}$ kg
11. 2000 g = 2 kg
12. 750 g = $\frac{3}{4}$ kg
13. 1500 g = $1\frac{1}{2}$ kg
14. 2750 g = $2\frac{3}{4}$ kg

Page 27
Grams and kilograms

1. 650 g = 0·65 kg 'example'
2. 250 g = 0·25 kg
3. 470 g = 0·47 kg
4. 1010 g = 1·01 kg
5. 1250 g = 1·25 kg
6. 870 g = 0·87 kg
7. 1650 g = 1·65 kg
8. 720 g = 0·72 kg
9. 800 g → 1 kg 'example'
10. 450 g → $\frac{1}{2}$ kg
11. 900 g → 1 kg
12. 600 kg → $\frac{1}{2}$ kg
13. 200 g → 0 kg
14. 700 g → 1 kg
15. 300 g → $\frac{1}{2}$ kg
16. 100 g → 0 kg
Rocket $\frac{1}{8}$ kg = 125 g; $\frac{1}{5}$ kg = 200 g; other answers will vary.

Page 28
Kilograms and grams

1. 942 g = 0·942 kg 'example'
2. 705 g = 0·705 kg
3. 1704 g = 1·704 kg
4. 1900 g = 1·9 kg
5. 812 g = 0·812 kg
6. 1010 g = 1·01 kg
7. 1235 g = 1·235 kg
8. 46 g = 0·046 kg
9. 70 g = 0·07 kg
10. 2030 g 'example'
11. 3104 g
12. 1002 g
13. 4050 g
14. 6009 g
15. 850 g
Rocket Answers will vary.

Page 29
Capacity

1. (a) 250 ml 'example'
   (d) 500 ml
   (e) 100 ml
   (g) $\frac{3}{4}$ l or 750 ml
   (h) 600 ml
   Containers that hold less than half a litre: (a), (e)
Rocket 4
2. $\frac{1}{2}$ l
3. $\frac{1}{4}$ l
4. 1 l
5. $\frac{3}{4}$ l
6. 1 l
7. 550 ml

Page 30
Capacity

1. $\frac{1}{2}$ l = 500 ml 'example'
2. $1\frac{1}{4}$ l = 1250 ml
3. $\frac{1}{4}$ l = 250 ml
4. $\frac{3}{4}$ l = 750 ml
5. $1\frac{1}{2}$ l = 1500 ml
6. $1\frac{3}{4}$ l = 1750 ml
7. 1 l = 1000 ml
8. 2 l = 2000 ml
Rocket 50 and 100

9. a and h 500 ml 'example'
b and f 200 ml
c and e 700 ml
d and g 800 ml

Page 31
Capacity

1. $\frac{1}{2}$ l = 500 ml 'example'
2. $\frac{3}{4}$ l = 750 ml
3. $\frac{1}{10}$ l = 100 ml
4. $\frac{1}{5}$ l = 200 ml
5. $\frac{1}{4}$ l = 250 ml
6. $\frac{1}{20}$ l = 50 ml
7. $\frac{1}{20}$ l, $\frac{1}{10}$ l, $\frac{1}{5}$ l, $\frac{1}{4}$ l, $\frac{1}{2}$ l, $\frac{3}{4}$ l
8. 500 ml = $\frac{1}{2}$ l
9. 400 ml = $\frac{4}{10}$ l or $\frac{2}{5}$ l
10. 250 ml = $\frac{1}{4}$ l
11. 100 ml = $\frac{1}{10}$ l
12. 750 ml = $\frac{3}{4}$ l
13. 1250 ml = $1\frac{1}{4}$ l
14. 1500 ml = $1\frac{1}{2}$ l
15. 1750 ml = $1\frac{3}{4}$ l

Rocket Answers will vary.

Page 32
Litres and millilitres

1. 100 ml = $\frac{1}{10}$ l 'example'
2. 500 ml = $\frac{5}{10}$ l or $\frac{1}{2}$ l
3. 250 ml = $\frac{1}{4}$ l
4. 200 ml = $\frac{2}{10}$ l or $\frac{1}{5}$ l
5. 750 ml = $\frac{3}{4}$ l
6. 50 ml = $\frac{1}{20}$ l
7. 1·5 l = $1\frac{1}{2}$ litres
8. 1·75 l = $1\frac{3}{4}$ litres
9. 1·25 l = $1\frac{1}{4}$ litres
10. 1·1 l = $1\frac{1}{10}$ litres
11. 2·25 l = $2\frac{1}{4}$ litres
12. 3·75 l = $3\frac{3}{4}$ litres
13. 750 ml
14. 850 ml
15. 300 ml
16. 1500 ml
17. 500 ml
18. 800 ml

Rocket One container holds 225 ml and the other holds 525 ml.

Page 33
Volume

1. 8·8 gallons 'example'
2. 22 gallons
3. 4·4 gallons
4. 13·2 gallons
5. 6·6 gallons
6. 1·1 gallons
7. 285 ml 'example'
8. 1425 ml or 1·425 l
9. 3990 ml or 3·9 l
10. 5700 ml or 5·7 l

Rocket Answers will vary but approximate amounts are 2-3 l or 4-6 pints.

Page 34
Area

1. Area = 15 cm² 'example'
2. Area = 8 cm²
3. Area = 24 cm²
4. Area = 16 cm²
5. Area = 30 cm²
6. Area = 21 cm²
7. Area = 24 cm²
8. Area = 11 cm²

Rocket Answers will vary.

Page 35
Perimeter

1. P = 24 + 40 = 64 cm 'example'
2. P = 36 + 44 = 80 cm
3. P = 60 + 90 = 150 cm
4. P = 36 + 56 = 92 cm
5. P = 84 + 40 = 124 cm
6. P = 9 + 7·4 = 16·4 m
7. P = 4·6 + 8·6 = 13·2 m
8. P = 72 + 32 = 104 cm

Rocket If children stick to whole centimetres, the dimensions will range from 1 cm × 17 cm (the 'longest' rectangle) to 6 cm × 6 cm (a square and so the 'shortest' rectangle).

9. 26 cm
10. 20 cm
11. 32 cm
12. 17 cm

Rocket 20 cm.

Page 36
Area

1. Area = 8 cm × 6 cm = 48 cm² 'example'
2. Area = 7 cm × 9 cm = 63 cm²
3. Area = 12 cm × 8 cm = 96 cm²
4. Area = 6 cm × 3 cm = 18 cm²
5. Area = 20 cm × 11 cm = 220 cm²
6. Area = 4 cm × 10 cm = 40 cm²
7. Area = 6 cm × 8·5 cm = 51 cm²
8. Area = 4·5 cm × 7 cm = 31·5 cm²
9. Area = 140 cm × 60 cm = 14 cm × 6 cm = 84 cm²

Rocket 7 cm
10. 19 m
11. 900 cm
12. £283·50

Page 37
Area

1–6. Answers will vary but could be:
1. square centimetres
2. square millimetres or square centimetres
3. square metres
4. square millimetres
5. square metres
6. square miles/kilometres/acres/hectares

Rocket Answers will vary.
7. 13 m × 40 m = 520 m² 'example'
8. 30 m × 15 m = 450 m²
9. 12 m × 18 m = 216 m²
10. 22 m × 11 m = 242 m²
11. 14 m × 20 m = 280 m²
12. 32 m × 14 m = 448 m²

Rocket Answers will vary.

Page 38
Estimate

1. 80 cm 'example'
2. 600 cm²
3. 150 cm²
4. 0·1 m
5. 50 cm
6. 40 cm²
7. 12 m²
8. Answers will vary.

Page 39
Perimeter

1. P = 35 cm
2. P = 26 cm
3. P = 27 cm
4. P = 22 cm
5. P = 16 mm
6. P = 16 cm

Rocket Triangle with sides 20 cm; square with sides 15 cm; pentagon with sides 12 cm; hexagon with sides 10 cm; decagon with sides 6 cm; dodecagon (12 sides) with sides 5 cm; 15-sided polygon with sides 4 cm; 20-sided polygon with sides 3 cm.

7. 6 cm by 8 cm
8. 49 cm²
9. 92 cm

Page 40
Perimeters

1. 14 cm 'example'
2. 14·2 cm
3. 31 cm
4. 38 cm
5. 52 cm
6. 116 cm
7. 310 cm or 3·1 m

Rocket Answers will vary. The longest possible perimeter is 12 units and the shortest is 10 units.

Page 41
Perimeter

1. 9 m
2. True
3. The perimeters of both blue shapes are the same. The same is true of the red shapes.

4. a = 3 units
b = 6 units
c = 4 units

5. a = 5 units
b = 4 units
c = 2 units

6. a = 2 units 'example'
b = 4 units
c = 1 units

Page 42
Areas of rectangular shapes

1. $21\,m^2$
2. $69\,m^2$
3. $74\,m^2$
4. $147\,m^2$
5. $118\,m^2$
6. $610\,m^2$
7. $6\,m \times 20\,m = 120\,m^2$
8. $44\,m \times 18\,m = 792\,m^2$
$792\,m^2 - 120\,m^2 = 672\,m^2$
9. $50\,m \times 80\,m = 4000\,m^2$
$4000\,m^2 - 792\,m^2 = 3208\,m^2$
10. $3208\,m^2 \times 2 = 6416\,m^2$
11. $100\,m \times 18\,m = 1800\,m^2$
12. $8000\,m^2 - 120\,m^2 = 7880\,m^2$

Page 43
Areas of rectangles

1. $128\,m^2$
2. $160\,m^2$
3. $119\,m^2$
4. $51\,m^2$
5. $248\,m^2$
6. $69{\cdot}5\,m^2$
7. $A = 28\,mm^2$
8. $L = 12\,cm$
9. $W = 50\,mm$ or $5\,cm$
10. $L = 6\,cm$
11. 2 cm and 6 cm
12. 6 cm and 4 cm
Rocket $16\,cm^2$ (the shape is a square).

Page 44
Areas of right-angled triangles

1. $6 \times 8 = 48$
Area $= 24\,cm^2$ 'example'
2. $9 \times 5 = 45$
Area $= 22{\cdot}5\,cm^2$
3. $8 \times 12 = 96$
Area $= 48\,cm^2$
4. $8 \times 8 = 64$
Area $= 32\,cm^2$
5. $6 \times 8{\cdot}5 = 51$
Area $= 25{\cdot}5\,cm^2$
6. $7 \times 8 = 56$
7. Area $= 28\,cm^2$
Rocket Area $= 8\,cm^2$
8. $A = 20$ units^2
9. $A = 10$ units^2
10. $A = 5$ units^2
11. $A = 12$ units^2

12. $A = 2$ units^2
13. $A = 3$ units^2
14. $A = 4{\cdot}5$ units^2
15. $A = 9$ units^2

Page 45
Areas of shapes that contain right-angled triangles

1. $A = 2\,cm^2$ 'example'
2. $A = 6\,cm^2$
3. $A = 7\,cm^2$
4. $A = 12\,cm^2$
5. $A = 8\,cm^2$
6. $A = 2\,cm^2$
7. $A = 6{\cdot}5\,cm^2$
8. $A = 2\,cm^2$
9. $A = 13{\cdot}5\,cm^2$
10. a = 4 cm 'example'
11. b = 6 cm
12. c = 9 cm
13. d = 8 cm
Rocket Answers will vary.

Page 46
Areas of non right-angled triangles

1. $3 \times 9 = 27$
$A = 13{\cdot}5\,cm^2$
$7 \times 9 = 63$
$A = 31{\cdot}5\,cm^2$
Total area $= 13{\cdot}5\,cm^2 + 31{\cdot}5\,cm^2 = 45\,cm^2$ 'example'
2. $3 \times 5 = 15$
$A = 7{\cdot}5\,cm^2$
$5 \times 6 = 30$
$A = 15\,cm^2$
Total area $= 7{\cdot}5\,cm^2 + 15\,cm^2 = 22{\cdot}5\,cm^2$
3. $7{\cdot}5 \times 4 = 30$
$A = 15\,cm^2$
$7{\cdot}5 \times 8 = 60$
$A = 30\,cm^2$
Total area $= 15\,cm^2 + 30\,cm^2 = 22{\cdot}5\,cm^2$
4. $8 \times 4 = 32$
$A = 16\,cm^2$
Total area $= 16\,cm^2 \times 2 = 32\,cm^2$
5. $6{\cdot}5 \times 12 = 78$
$A = 39\,cm^2$
$6{\cdot}5 \times 3 = 19{\cdot}5$
$A = 9{\cdot}75\,cm^2$
Total area $= 39\,cm^2 + 9{\cdot}75\,cm^2 = 48{\cdot}75\,cm^2$
6. Each area is $24\,cm^2$
Rocket Answers will vary.

Page 47
Solids

1. $4\,cm^3$ 'example'
2. $4\,cm^3$
3. $4\,cm^3$
4. $4\,cm^3$

5. red and yellow $8\,cm^3$ 'example'
6. blue and green $8\,cm^3$
7. red and green $8\,cm^3$
8. green and yellow $8\,cm^3$
9. $16\,cm^3$

Page 48
Surface area of cuboids

1. $(2 \times 9) + (2 \times 15) + (2 \times 15)$
$= 18 + 30 + 30 = 78\,cm^2$ 'example'
2. $(2 \times 8) + (2 \times 28) + (2 \times 14)$
$= 16 + 56 + 28 = 100\,cm^2$
3. $(2 \times 12) + (2 \times 24) + (2 \times 32)$
$= 24 + 48 + 64 = 136\,cm^2$
4. $(2 \times 15) + (2 \times 33) + (2 \times 55)$
$= 30 + 66 + 110 = 206\,cm^2$
5. $(2 \times 24) + (2 \times 32) + (2 \times 48)$
$= 48 + 64 + 96 = 208\,cm^2$
6. $(2 \times 21) + (2 \times 27) + (2 \times 63)$
$= 42 + 54 + 126 = 222\,cm^2$
Rocket The surface area is not always the same. With 5 cubes the largest is $22\,cm^2$ and the smallest is $20\,cm^2$.

Page 49
Volume

1. 22 cubes 'example'
2. 30 cubes
3. 20 cubes
4. 24 cubes
5. 20 cubes
6. 38 cubes
7. 44 cubes
8. 24 cubes
9. 24 cubes
Rocket Answers will vary.

Page 50
Scale

Child's drawings should measure:
1. 20 cm × 6 cm
2. 9 cm × 4 cm
3. 20 cm × 15 cm
4. 8 cm × 12 cm
5. 8 cm × 9 cm
6. 11 cm × 4 cm

Page 51
Scale

London and Birmingham are about 2 cm apart. That is 100 miles in reality. 'example'
Answers will vary.

Page 52
Scale

1–3. Pictures drawn to scale.
Rocket Answers will vary.

Page 53

Problems

1. 40 days. 10 days longer
2. 67
3. 780 l
4. 250
Rocket 1600 seconds or 26 minutes 40 seconds
5. 20 cm
6. 12 cm
7. 30 cm
8. 42 cm²
9. 12 cm²
10. 16 cm²

Page 54

Problems

1. 4 kg; 4·5 kg
2. 2·6 kg
3. 1·05 kg
4. 4 cm = 40 mm
   40 mm ÷ 100 = 0·4 mm 'example'
5. 7 cm = 70 mm
   70 mm ÷ 100 = 0·7 mm
6. 2 cm = 20 mm
   20 mm ÷ 100 = 0·2 mm
7. 5·4 cm = 54 mm
   54 mm ÷ 100 = 0·54 mm
8. 3·2 cm = 32 mm
   32 mm ÷ 100 = 0·32 mm
9. 6·1 cm = 61 mm
   61 mm ÷ 100 = 0·61 mm

Page 55

Measurement problems

1. 15·8 g. About $\frac{2}{3}$ of the GDA.
2. 20 g
3. $\frac{2}{9}$ of the GDA.
4. 0·9 g
5. 200 g
6. 1·6 g
Rocket Answers will vary.

Measure PPMs

PPM 219

Units of measure

1. Answers may vary but are most likely to be:
   g, 'example' l, ml
   km, g, cm,
   km, kg, mm
2. Answers will vary.

PPM 220

Millimetres, centimetres, metres and kilometers

1. 100 cm
2. 50 cm
3. 135 cm
4. 8 cm
5. 1 m
6. 5 m
7. 2 m
8. 1500 m
9. 20 mm
10. 5 mm
11. 1000 mm
12. 67 mm
13. 3500 mm
14. 2250 m
15. Answers will vary.

PPM 221

Weight

1. 1 kg
2. 500 g
3. 2000 g
4. 250 g
5. $\frac{3}{4}$ kg or 0·75 kg
6. $\frac{4}{10}$ kg or 0·4 kg
7. 100 g
8. 3750 g
9. 2300 g
10. 5800 g
11. $8\frac{1}{2}$ kg or 8·5 kg
12. 12 kg
13. 20 000 g
14. 1000 g
15. Answers will vary.

PPM 222

Litres and millilitres

1. 1000 ml
2. 500 ml
3. 2 l
4. 750 ml
5. 1500 ml
6. $\frac{1}{4}$ l or 0·25 l
7. $6\frac{1}{2}$ l or 6·5 l
8. 100 ml
9. 2700 ml
10. 5100 ml
11. 11 l
12. 2750 ml
13. 3500 ml
14. 10 000 ml
15. Answers will vary.

PPM 223

Units of measure

1. ounce, oz, weight; kilogram, kg, weight; gram, g, weight; millimetre, mm, length; litre, l, capacity; pound, lb, weight; millilitre, ml, capacity; inch, " or in, length; gallon, gal, capacity; centimeter, cm, length; foot, ' or ft, length; mile, m, length.
2. **Metric:** kilogram, gram, millimetre, litre, millilitre, centimetre.
   Imperial: ounce, pound, inch, gallon, foot, mile.
3. Answers will vary.

PPM 224

Estimating

1. 1 m
2. 2 m.
3–9. Answers will vary.

PPM 225

Area

1. doormat 'example'
   piece of toast
   chopping board
   saucer or postcard
   football pitch
   playground
   postcard
   computer screen or open book
   magazine cover
   bed sheet
   kitchen floor
   car park
2. Answers will vary.

PPM 226

Estimating length

1–12. Answers will vary.

PPM 227

Centimetres and inches

Answers will vary.

PPM 228

Estimating weights

1–4. Answers will vary.

PPM 229

Ordering weights

1. 1·4 kg 'example'
2. 1·3 kg
3. 2·1 kg
4. 5·1 kg
5. 3·5 kg
6. 6·2 kg
7. 0·75 kg
8. 10·1 kg
9. 9·9 kg
10. 0·75 kg, 1·3 kg, 1·4 kg, 2·1 kg, 3·5 kg, 5·1 kg, 6·2 kg, 9·9 kg, 10·1 kg
11. 1400 g, 1300 g, 2100 g, 5100 g, 3500 g, 6200 g, 750 g, 10 100 g, 9900 g

PPM 230

Weighing scales

1. 740 g
2. 370 g
3. 530 g

4. 2·6 kg or 2600 g
5. 6·4 kg or 6400 g
6. 1·7 kg or 1700 g
7. 3·8 kg or 3800 g
8. 4·4 kg or 4400 g
9. 9 kg
10. 7 kg
11. 6·5 kg or 6500 g
12. 16 kg or 16 000 g

PPM 231
Estimating capacities

1–4. Answers will vary.

PPM 232
Perimeters of rectangles

Estimates and differences will vary.
1. 126 mm
2. 156 mm
3. 108 mm
4. 150 mm
5. 146 mm
6. 162 mm
7. Answers will vary.

PPM 233
Area

1 and **2.** Answers will vary.

PPM 234
Perimeter

1. 50 cm, 520 cm
2. 40 cm, 420 cm
3. 18 cm, 304 cm
4. 330 cm
5. 112 cm
6. 258 cm
7. 136 cm
8. 260 cm
9. 300 cm

PPM 235
Areas of triangles

1. 10 cm^2
2. 9 cm^2
3. 13·5 cm^2
4. 4·5 cm^2
5. 37·5 cm^2
6. 21 cm^2
7. 27·5 cm^2

PPM 236
Areas of shapes

1. 2 cm^2 **2.** 1 cm^2
3. 4 cm^2 **4.** 2 cm^2
5. 3 cm^2 **6.** 1 cm^2
7. 2 cm^2 **8.** 3 cm^2
9. 1·5 cm^2 **10.** 3·5 cm^2
11. 2 cm^2 **12.** 3 cm^2

PPM 237
Cubes

Cube	Number of cubes	Surface area
1 × 1 × 1	1	6 cm^2
2 × 2 × 2	8	24 cm^2
3 × 3 × 3	27	54 cm^2
4 × 4 × 4	64	96 cm^2
5 × 5 × 5	125	150 cm^2
6 × 6 × 6	216	216 cm^2
10 × 10 × 10	1000	600 cm^2

Answers about the patterns may vary. A possible answer is: surface area = number of cubes × (6 / length).

PPM 238
Volume and surface area

1. 24 cm^3, 'example' 56 cm^2
2. 24 cm^3, 56 cm^2
3. 24 cm^3, 70 cm^2
4. 36 cm^3, 66 cm^2
5. 36 cm^3, 72 cm^2
6. 36 cm^3, 98 cm^2
7. Cuboids with the same volume do not necessarily have the same surface area.
8. The more flattened a shape the greater the surface area. More compact shapes (i.e. those tending towards cubes and spheres) have the lowest surface area to volume ratio.

PPM 239
Tennis court

1. a) 24 m   b) 11 m
     c) 8 m   d) 6·5 m
     e) 4 m
2. The drawing would be smaller.

PPM 240
Kilometres and miles

Answers should be close to the following:
1. 80
2. 115
3. 83
4. 99
5. 619
6. 152
7. 554
8. 1029
9. 352
10. 298

PPM 241
Inches and centimeters

1 and **2.** Answers will vary.

PPM 242
Measure problems

1. 50
2. 16
3. 4
4. 1680 miles

PPM 243
Measurement problems

1. 4·25 m, 2·5 m
2–4. Answers will vary.

Shape, Position and Movement Pupil Book 6

Page 3
3D objects

1. cube 'example'
2. triangular-based pyramid or tetrahedron
3. square-based pyramid
4. triangular prism
5. cuboid
6. pentagon-based pyramid
Rocket 8, 10, 11

Page 4
Octahedrons

1. No 'example'
2. Yes
3. Yes
4. Yes
5. Yes
6. Yes
7. Yes
8. No
9. Yes

Page 5
3D objects

1. cube 'example'
2. cuboid
3. none
4. square-based pyramid
5. none
6. cube
7. none
8. prism
9. none
10–12. Answers may vary.

Page 6
Angles

1. 2 right angles 'example'
2. 3 right angles
3. 1 right angle
4. 2 right angles
5. 2 right angles

6. 1 right angle
7. 1 right angle
Number of degrees:
1. 180°
2. 270°
3. 90°
4. 180°
5. 180°
6. 90°
7. 90°
8. 2 right angles
9. 2 right angles
10. 3 right angles
11. 1 right angle
Turning anti-clockwise:
8. 2 right angles
9. 2 right angles
10. 1 right angle
11. 3 right angles
Rocket Answers will vary.

Page 7
Angles

1. South 'example'
2. South
3. North-east
4. North-west
5. North
6. South-east
7. 180° 'example'
8. 270°
9. 90°
10. 360°
Rocket 8 ways

Page 8
Direction

1. North 'example'
2. East
3. West
4. South
5. North-east
6. South-east
7. North-west
8. South-west
Rocket North and South
East and West
North-east and South-west
North-west and South-east
9. Riptide 'example'
10. Surf Central
11. Deluge
12. Super Slide
13. Surf Central
14. Rapids

Page 9
Direction

1. South-east 'example'
2. North-east
3. East
4. North

5. North
6. South
7. North-east
8. West
Rocket Answers will vary.

Page 10
Angles

1. 180° 'example'
2. 90°
3. 270°
4. 45°
5. 135°
6. 225°
7. 90°
8. 315°
9. SE 'example'
10. N
11. S
12. NE
13. NW
14. W
15. E
16. SW
17. NE
Rocket N, SW, NE, W, S, SE, NW, E, W

Page 11
Angles

1. 90° 'example'
2. 225°
3. 135°
4. 45°
5. 315°
6. 90°
7. 135°
8. 90°
9. 45°
10. 45° 'example'
11. 90°
12. 135°
13. 180°
14. 225°
15. 270°
Rocket Answers will vary.

Page 12
Coordinates

Inverness (4, 9)
Dundee (5, 8)
Edinburgh (5, 7)
Glasgow (4, 7)
Newcastle (6, 6)
Lancaster (5, 5)
York (6, 5)
Hull (7, 5)
Nottingham (6, 4)
Aberystwyth (4, 3)
Birmingham (6, 3)
London (7, 2)
Dover (8, 2)
Bristol (5, 2) 'example'

Plymouth (4, 1)
Rocket York, Hull, Nottingham, Aberystwyth, Birmingham, London, Dover, Bristol, Plymouth

Page 13
Coordinates

1. (2, 1), (2, 5), (5, 1)
2. (1, 1), (3, 6), (4, 1), (6, 6)
3.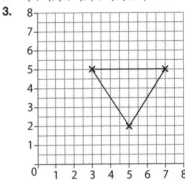
4.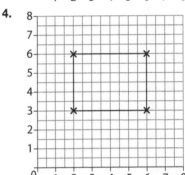
5.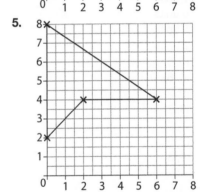
6.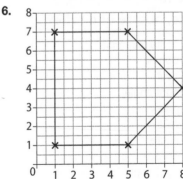
Rocket Answers will vary.
Rocket Answers will vary.

Page 14
Coordinates

1. (4, 5) 'example'
2. (5, 0)
3. 3

4. 1
5. 0
6. 2
7. 3
8. 7
9. 1
10. 2
11. Shorton and Forton
12. Gorle and Thwaite
13. Forton
14. Bigby
15. Gorle
16. Arndale
17. Forton
18. Forton

Page 15
Coordinates

1. A (2, 2) 'example'
   B (5, 2)
   C (6, 5)
   D (3, 4)
   E (4, 6)
   F (7, 8)
   G (8, 3)
   H (7, 2)
   I (8, 6)
   J (2, 8)
   K (0, 3)
   L (5, 9)
   M (3, 6)
2. 7 units
3. 6 units
4. 5 units
5. 2 units
6. (5, 6)
7. (6, 8)
8. (0, 2)
9. (9, 2)
10. (6, 2)
11. (7, 5)
12. (3, 5)

Page 16
Acute, obtuse and reflex

1. acute 'example'
2. obtuse
3. acute
4. right angle
5. reflex
6. reflex
7. acute
8. obtuse
9. right angle
10. a) acute 'example' b) obtuse
    c) acute d) obtuse
11. e) acute f) acute g) acute
12. h) obtuse i) obtuse j) acute
    k) obtuse l) obtuse
13. m) obtuse n) acute o) obtuse
    p) obtuse
14. q) right angle r) acute s) reflex
    t) acute u) right angle

15. v) acute w) acute x) acute y) reflex
Rocket false; true; true

Page 17
Acute, obtuse and reflex

Pinboard	Acute	Right angle	Obtuse	Reflex
1	2	1	0	0
2	3	0	0	0
3	3	0	0	0
4	2	1	0	0
5	2	0	1	0
6	2	1	0	0
7	2	0	1	0
8	2	1	0	0
9	3	0	0	1
10	1	2	1	0
11	0	4	0	0
12	2	0	2	0
13	2	1	1	0
14	1	2	1	0
15	2	0	2	0

Rocket Answers will vary but children may observe that the internal angles always add up to 540°.

Page 18
Angles

1. 60° 'example'
2. 20°
3. 130°
4. 80°
5. 170°
6. 150°
7. a) Answers will vary.
   b) 25°
8. a) Answers will vary.
   b) 58°
9. a) Answers will vary.
   b) 86°
10. a) Answers will vary.
    b) 70°
Rocket 3 slices: 120°; 4 slices: 90°;
5 slices: 72°; 6 slices: 60°;
8 slices: 45°; 9 slices: 40°;
10 slices: 36°

Page 19
Angles

Answers 1–6 are only approximate.
1. 35° 'example'
2. 58°
3. 125°
4. 39°
5. 92°
6. 95°
Estimates will vary.
7. a) 29° b) 120° c) 320°
Rocket Answers will vary.

Page 20
Angles

1. 105°, 75°
2. 60°, 120°
3. 150°, 30°
4. 75°, 105°
5. 67·5°, 112·5°
6. 135°, 45°
Rocket Any point on the line from (0, 0) to (6, 3) will make the same angle with the x-axis: (1, 0·5), (2, 1), (3, 1·5) and so on. Children may notice that for this line the x value is always double the y value.

Page 21
Angles in a triangle

1. a = 40°, b = 70°, c = 70°
2. a = 45°, b = 90°, c = 45°
3. a = 60°, b = 60°, c = 60°
4. a = 22·5°, b = 135°, c = 22·5°
5. They all add up to 180
6. Diagrams will vary. Children should notice that the angles total 360°.

Page 22
Angles

1–6. Answers will vary.
Rocket Answers will vary.
7. Straight line
8. Straight line
9. Not a straight line
10. Not a straight line
11. Straight line
12. Straight line

Page 23
Drawing angles

1–6. Angles drawn correctly.
Rocket Answers will vary.
7. Full turn.
8. Not a full turn.
9. Full turn.
10. Not a full turn.
11. Full turn.
12. Full turn.

Page 24
Parallel and perpendicular

1. Does the shape have parallel sides:
   a) Yes: 1 pair 'example'
   b) Yes: 3 pairs
   c) Yes: 1 pair
   d) Yes: 3 pairs
   e) Yes: 2 pairs
   f) Yes: 2 pairs
   g) Yes: 2 pairs
   h) Yes: 1 pair
   i) No
   j) No
   k) No
   l) Yes: 3 pairs
2. Does the shape have perpendicular sides:
   a) Yes
   b) Yes
   c) Yes
   d) Yes
   e) No
   f) Yes
   g) Yes
   h) Yes
   i) Yes
   j) Yes
   k) No
   l) No
Rocket Answers will vary.

Page 25
Parallel and perpendicular

1. d
2. l and n
3. p
4. b and d
5. i
6. a
7. l and n
8. e
9. q
10. g
11. b
12. s
Rocket Answers will vary.
13. True
14. True
Rocket Answers will vary.

Page 26
Triangles

1. a, e, g
2. b, c, d, f, h
3. a, e, g
4. b, c, d, f, h
5. b, c, e, g
6. a, d, f, h
7. a, e, g
8. b, c, e, g
9. d, f, h
10. a
11. Answers will vary.
12. true
13. false
14. true
15. false

Page 27
Triangles

1. a) right-angled scalene 'example'
   b) isosceles
   c) right-angled isosceles
   d) scalene
   e) scalene
   f) right-angled scalene
   g) isosceles
   h) isosceles
   i) right-angled isosceles
   j) isosceles
   k) scalene
   l) scalene
2. b, c, g, h, i, j
Rocket Answers will vary.
Venn diagram
3. b, g, h, j
4. a, f
5. c, i
6. d, e, k, l

Page 28
Polygons

1. a) Yes 'example'
   b) Yes
   c) No
   d) Yes
   e) Yes
   f) No
   g) Yes
   h) Yes
2. b, e, h
3. a, d, g
4. a)

   b)

c)
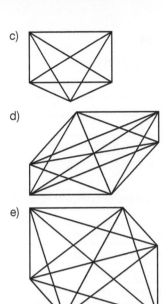
d)

e)

f)
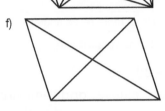

5. a) rectangle 'example'
   b) rectangle
   c) pentagon
   d) hexagon
   e) octagon
   f) quadrilateral/parallelogram
6. a) 2
   b) 2
   c) 5
   d) 9
   e) 9
   f) 2

Page 29

Quadrilaterals

1.

	square	rectangle	parallelogram	rhombus	trapezium	kite	arrowhead
Has 4 sides	green	green	green	green	green	green	green
Has all sides the same length	green	red	red	green	red	red	red
Has one pair of opposite sides parallel	red	red	red	red	green	red	red
Has two pairs of opposite sides parallel	green	green	green	green	red	red	red
Has opposite sides equal	green	green	green	green	yellow	red	red
Has adjacent sides equal	green	red	red	green	yellow	green	green
Has line symmetry	green	green	red	green	yellow	green	green
Has a right angle	green	green	yellow	red	yellow	yellow	yellow
Has an obtuse angle	red	red	yellow	green	green	green	yellow
Has one or more reflex angles	red	red	red	red	red	red	green

Rocket Answers will vary.

Page 30

Circles, ellipses and semi-circles

1. a, d, f, h
2. b, e, g
3. a, c, f, i
4. Answers will vary.

Page 31

Circles

1. circumference 'example'
2. radius
3. diameter
4. circle
5. radius
6. semi-circle
7. chord
8. sector
9. sector
10. segment
11. segment
12. chord
Rocket The triangles will always be isosceles but the apex can contain any angle under 180° including 90°.

Page 32

3D objects

1. a) prism or triangular prism
b) 6 vertices
c) 9 edges
d) 5 faces
2. a) pyramid or triangular-based pyramid
b) 4 vertices
c) 6 edges
d) 4 faces
3. a) cube or hexahedron
b) 8 vertices
c) 12 edges
d) 6 faces

4. a) cuboid
b) 8 vertices
c) 12 edges
d) 6 faces
5. a) cuboid
b) 8 vertices
c) 12 edges
d) 6 faces
6. a) pyramid or hexagonal pyramid
b) 7 vertices
c) 12 edges
d) 7 faces
7. a) prism or hexagonal prism
b) 12 vertices
c) 18 edges
d) 8 faces
8. a) pyramid or square-based pyramid
b) 5 vertices
c) 8 edges
d) 5 faces
9. a) prism or pentagonal prism
b) 10 vertices
c) 15 edges
d) 7 faces
10. a) tetrahedron or triangular-based pyramid
b) 4 vertices
c) 6 edges
d) 4 faces
11. a) prism or triangular prism
b) 6 vertices
c) 9 edges
d) 5 faces
12. a) octahedron
b) 6 vertices
c) 12 edges
d) 8 faces
Rocket Answers will vary.

Page 33

3D objects

1. cube 6 faces
2. tetrahedron 4 faces

3. triangular prism 5 faces
4. pentagonal prism 7 faces
5. cuboid 6 faces
6. square-based pyramid 5 faces
7. hexagonal prism 8 faces
8. 'example'

9.

10.

11.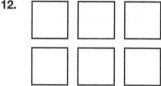

12.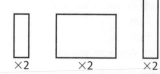

Rocket Answers will vary.

Page 34

3D objects

1. Cuboid 'example'
6 faces

×2	×2	×2
rectangle	rectangle	rectangle

2. Tetrahedron
4 faces

×4
triangle

3. Octahedron
8 faces

×8
triangle

4. Triangular prism
5 faces

×2　　　　×3
triangle　　rectangle

5. Hexagonal prism
8 faces

 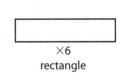
×2　　　　　×6
hexagon　　　rectangle

6. Square-based pyramid
5 faces

×1　　　　×4
square　　triangle

1. a) yes　b) yes　c) yes　d) yes
2. a) no　b) no　c) no　d) no
3. a) yes　b) no　c) yes　d) yes
4. a) yes　b) yes　c) yes　d) yes
5. a) yes　b) yes　c) yes　d) yes
6. a) no　b) no　c) yes　d) yes
Rocket Triangular or pentagonal prisms would fit the description, as would any prisms whose cross-section has an odd number of sides.

Page 35
Objects with curved faces

1. c, e, h, i
2. j, k, l
3. b, f, l
4. e, h, i, l
5. Answers will vary.

Page 36
Nets of cones and cylinders

Net 1 → Shape B 'example'
Net 2 → Shape E
Net 3 → Shape F
Net 4 → Shape D
Net 5 → Shape C
Net 6 → Shape A

Page 37
Combining shapes

1. regular hexagon 'example'
2. equilateral triangle
3. trapezium

4. parallelogram
5. rhombus
6. irregular pentagon
7. Answers will vary but should include six of these:

8. Answers will vary.

Page 38
Tessellating

Answers will vary.

Page 39
Angles in tessellations

1. regular hexagons
Yellow angle = 120° 'example'
2. regular octagons and squares
Yellow angle = 135°
3. regular hexagons, equilateral triangles and squares
Yellow angle = 120°
4. regular dodecagons and equilateral triangles
Yellow angle = 150°
5. kites and isosceles triangles
Yellow angle = 45°
6. squares, trapeziums and equilateral triangles
Yellow angle = 120°
7. irregular decagons and equilateral triangles
Yellow angle = 240°
Rocket Answers will vary.

Page 40
Symmetry

1.
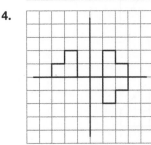

2.
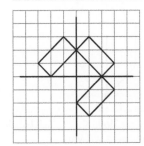

3.

4.

5. 1
6. 2
7. 0
8. 4
9. Answers will vary.
Rocket Answers will vary but children may notice that some patterns produce the same result whether rotated or reflected across two axes, as in the example shown.

Page 41
Reflections

1.
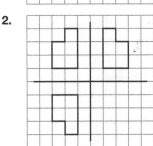

2.
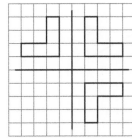

3.

4.
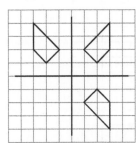

5.

Shape, position and Movement Pupil Book 6

6.

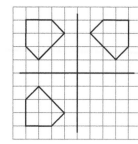

Rocket Answers will vary.

Page 42
Rotations

1.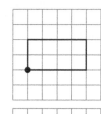

2.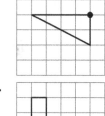

3.

4.

5.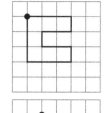

6.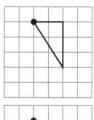

7.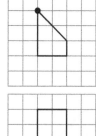

8.

9. a **10.** c **11.** a
Rocket Answers will vary.

26

Page 43
Rotations

1. a)

b)

c)

d)

2. a)

b)

c)

d)

3. a)

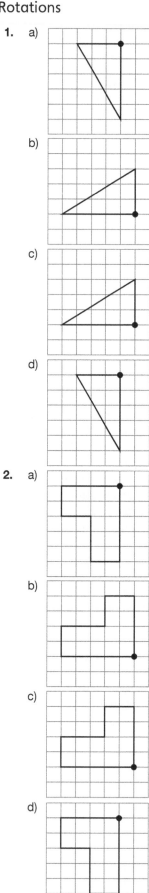

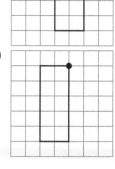

b)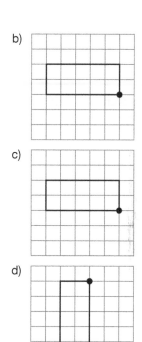

c)

d)

Rocket After 90° clockwise, A is at (6, 3)
B is at (5, 3) C is at (5, 2)
After 180° clockwise, A is at
(3, 2) B is at (3, 3) C is at (2, 3)
After 270° clockwise, A is at
(2, 5) B is at (3, 5) C is at (3, 6)

Page 44
Patterns

1. a)

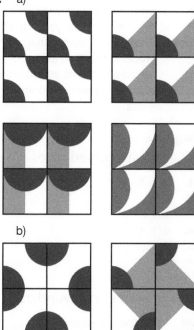

b)

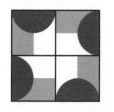

c)

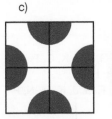

 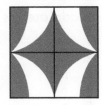

Rocket Answers will vary.

Page 45
Polygons

1.
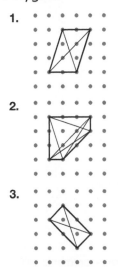

2.

3.

1. quadrilateral, 2 diagonals
2. pentagon, 5 diagonals
3. rectangle, 2 diagonals
4. pentagon 5 diagonals; hexagon 9 diagonals

Rocket All hexagons have the same number of diagonals because they all have the same number of vertices to join up.

5. true
6. true
7. true
8. true
9. true
10. true
11. true
12. true
13. true

Page 46
Triangles

1. Ways of describing triangles will vary but should be along these lines:
   a) 1 medium, 4 small 'example'
   b) 1 big, 3 medium, 9 small
   c) 1 large, 3 big, 6 medium, 16 small

Rocket 1 very large, 3 large, 6 big, 10 medium, 25 small

Rocket Answers will vary.

Page 47
Quadrilaterals

Rocket Answers will vary.
1. true
2. true
3. true
4. true
5. true
6. false
7. true
8. true
9. false
10. false
11. true
12. true

Rocket The diagonals always cut each other in half.

Shape, Position and Movement PPMs

PPM 244
Nets

1.
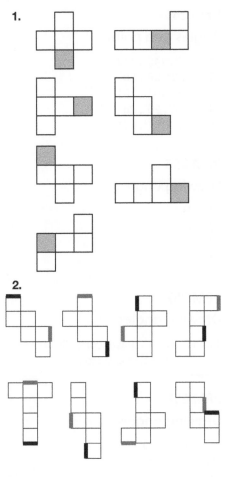

2.

PPM 245
Degrees

1. 90°
2. 270°
3. 180°

4. 90°
5. 360°
6. 270°
7. 180°
8. 270°
9. 90°

PPM 246
Degrees

1. TERM
2. SIGN
3. COLD
4. METRE
5. SINGING

PPM 247
Compass directions

1. N 'example'
2. W
3. S
4. SE
5. E
6. NE
7. NW
8. W
9. SW
10. SE

PPM 248
Compass directions

1. House
2. Train
3. Flag or house
4. Windmill
5. Tree
6. Castle
7. Cart or bicycle
8. Windmill

PPM 249
Coordinates

1. square
2. triangle
3. pentagon
4. circle
5. rectangle
6. hexagon
7. square
8. triangle
9. hexagon
10. circle

PPM 250
Coordinates

A (3, 1)
B (2, 4)
C (7, 5)
D (1, 2)
E (8, 0)

F (6, 2)
G (4, 6)
H (1, 8)
I (0, 5)
J (5, 3)

PPM 251

Types of angles

1. acute 'example'
2. right
3. reflex
4. obtuse
5. straight
6. acute
7. Answers will vary.

PPM 252

Acute, obtuse, and reflex angles

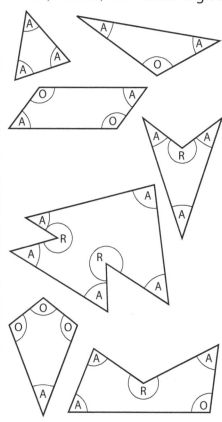

PPM 253

Angles of polygons

Answers will vary but could be as shown:

Example of a triangle with 1 obtuse and 2 acute angles.

Example of a quadrilateral with 2 obtuse and 2 acute angles.

Example of a quadrilateral with 1 reflex and 3 acute angles.

Example of a pentagon with 2 right angles, 2 obtuse and 1 acute angle.

PPM 254

Estimating and measuring angles

Estimates and differences will vary. Actual measurements are as shown.
a) 127°
b) 42°
c) 153°
d) 74°
e) 30°
f) 100°
g) 62°

PPM 255

Angles at a point

1. 38°, 142°, 142°
2. 122°, 58°, 58°
3. 79°, 101°, 101°
4. 154°, 26°, 26°
5. 29°, 151°, 151°

PPM 256

Drawing angles

1. B
2. C
3. E
4. F

PPM 257

Drawing angles

1 and 2. Angles drawn correctly on circles, in any order.

PPM 258

Drawing angles

1. Aberness
2. Killidagen
3. Mcfaedon
4. Coldport

PPM 259

Triangles

Right-angled – C, G, H, I, K, O, P
Isosceles – A, E, H, I L, O
Scalene – B, C, D, F, G, J, K, M, N, P

PPM 260

Quadrilaterals

1. r
2. t
3. p
4. p
5. s
6. t
7. t
8. p
9. t
10. p
11. s
12. p
13. t
14. r
15. t
16. p

PPM 261

Polygons

1–16. Answers may vary.

PPM 262

Circles

1 and 2. Children's measurements will approximate to the following.

	Length of diameter	Length of circumference	Circumference /diameter
Circle a	7 cm	22 cm	3·14
Circle b	5 cm	15·7 cm	3·14
Circle c	4 cm	12·6 cm	3·14
Circle d	6 cm	18·8 cm	3·14

3. Children should notice that the answer to the division is always approximately 3·1 or 3·14.

PPM 263

Circles again

1. Children should notice that the angles are always approximately 90°.
2. Answers will vary.

PPM 264

3D objects

1–6. Answers will vary.

PPM 265
3D objects

1.

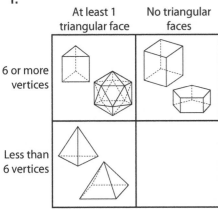

	At least 1 triangular face	No triangular faces
6 or more vertices		
Less than 6 vertices		

PPM 266
3D objects

1.

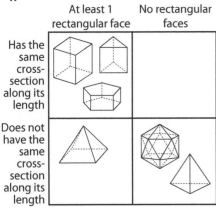

	At least 1 rectangular face	No rectangular faces
Has the same cross-section along its length		
Does not have the same cross-section along its length		

PPM 267
Drawing cuboids

Answers will vary.

PPM 268
Sorting shapes

1.

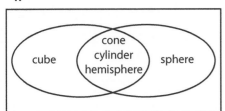

2.

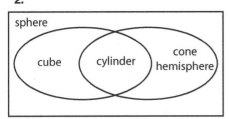

3.

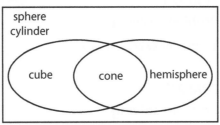

PPM 269
Cross-sections

1. true
2. true
3. false
4. true
5. true
6. true
7. true
8. false
9. Answers will vary.

PPM 270
Shapes

1.   'example'

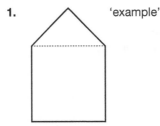

Answers will vary but could be as follows:

2.

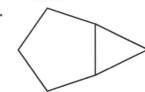

3.

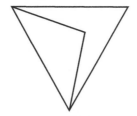

4.

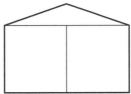

5.

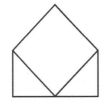

6.

7.

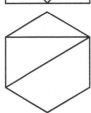

8.

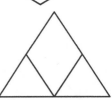

9.

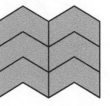

10. Answers will vary.

PPM 271
Tessellating

1. This shape tessellates.

This shape tessellates.

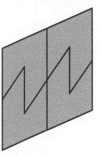

This shape does not tessellate.

This shape tessellates.

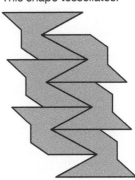

2. Answers will vary.

PPM 272
Reflection

mirror

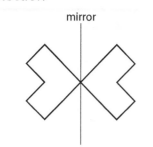

mirror

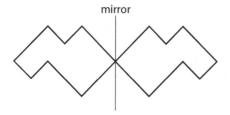

mirror

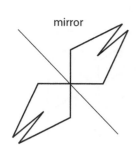

PPM 273
Reflecting and rotating

1–4. Answers will vary.

PPM 274
Problem solving

1 and **2.** Answers will vary.

PPM 275
Problem solving

1. 6 grey 0 white 'example'
2. 10 grey 2 white 'example'
3. 14 grey 4 white
4. 18 grey 6 white
5. 16 grey 8 white
6. 22 grey 14 white
7. 28 grey 20 white
8. 34 grey 26 white
9. Answers will vary.

PPM 276
Problem solving

1. $a = 140°$ 'example'
2. $b = 120°$
3. $c = 135°$
4. $d = 30°$
5. $e = 30°$
6. $f = 105°$
7. Answers will vary.

PPM 277
Circles

1–4. Answers will vary.

Part of Pearson

Author Team: Lynda Keith, Hilary Koll and Steve Mills

Heinemann is an imprint of Pearson Education Limited, a company incorporated in England and Wales, having its registered office at Edinburgh Gate, Harlow, Essex, CM20 2JE. Registered company number: 872828

www.pearsonschools.co.uk

Heinemann is a registered trademark of Pearson Education Limited

Text © Pearson Education Limited 2011

First published 2011
20 19 18 17
10 9 8 7 6 5 4

British Library Cataloguing in Publication Data
A catalogue record for this book is available from the British Library

ISBN 978 0 435 047887

Typeset by Tech-Set Ltd, Gateshead
Cover design by Pearson Education Limited
Cover illustration Volker Beisler © Pearson Education Limited
Printed in the UK by Henry Ling Ltd.

Acknowledgements
Every effort has been made to contact copyright holders of material reproduced in this book. Any omissions will be rectified in subsequent printings if notice is given to the publishers.